THE PORTAGE POETRY SERIES

Listening to Mars
Sally Ashton

Glitter City
Bonnie Jill Emanuel

The Trouble with Being a Childless Only Child
Michelle Meyer

Happy Everything
Caitlin Cowan

Dear Lo
Brady Bove

Sadness of the Apex Predator
Dion O'Reilly

Do Not Feed the Animal
Hikari Miya

The Watching Sky
Judy Brackett Crowe

Let It Be Told in a Single Breath
Russell Thorburn

The Blue Divide
Linda Nemec Foster

Lake, River, Mountain
Mark B. Hamilton

Talking Diamonds
Linda Nemec Foster

Poetic People Power
Tara Bracco (ed.)

The Green Vault Heist
David Salner

The Stone Tries to Understand the Hands

"*The Stone Tries to Understand the Hands* is a dazzling book of poems—I underlined many lines and images. The electric particulars of the past and the sorrow of knowing dovetail into poems that pulse with music, pleasure. One of the greatest pleasures is the lyrical thinking that serpentines through the language. Another pleasure: the attentiveness to other texts, to language itself. This is a book with a wondrous reach, but it never loses sight of human intimacies and intricacies. Susannah Sheffer is a tremendously gifted poet. Her poems are deftly crafted, luminous."

—EDUARDO C. CORRAL
author of *Guillotine*

"These deep, clear, open-hearted poems unfold into stories about love and loss, growth, responsibility, hope. The intelligence underlying them is like some simple but profound invention—the wheel, perhaps, or fire. These are poems to return to again and again. They will go on booming in your heart after you close the book."

—POLLY SHULMAN
author of the *Grimm Legacy* series

"These are wonderful, enticing poems, tightly bursting with new meanings. We readers are bestowed with fascinating explorations of the relationship of objects and humans, the intimate touch between them. Through the stone, glass, stick, and cup we are invited to dive into a supra-animated world with layers of affinities. I loved reading this strong, original collection."

—SUZANNE E. BERGER
author of *Horizontal Woman*

"I told myself I'd read a few poems and ended up reading the whole book in one sitting. These poems are spare and deeply felt. They are at ease with themselves, both surprising and strikingly honest, each one a separate light radiating from a hand closed to protect what it holds. The only way to hear these poems is to keep on exploring the facets of desire that light them up, let them take us right here, into the center of our lives. 'Tell me if you have any better ideas,' says the final line in this splendid collection."

—FLEDA BROWN
author of *Flying Through a Hole in the Storm*

The Stone Tries to Understand the Hands

poems

Susannah Sheffer

CORNERSTONE PRESS
UNIVERSITY OF WISCONSIN-STEVENS POINT

Cornerstone Press, Stevens Point, Wisconsin 54481
Copyright © 2025 Susannah Sheffer
www.uwsp.edu/cornerstone

Printed in the United States of America by
Point Print and Design Studio, Stevens Point, Wisconsin

Library of Congress Control Number: 2024947454
ISBN: 978-1-960329-61-5

Cornerstone Press titles are produced in courses and internships offered by the
Department of English at the University of Wisconsin–Stevens Point.

DIRECTOR & PUBLISHER
Dr. Ross K. Tangedal

EXECUTIVE EDITORS
Jeff Snowbarger, Freesia McKee

EDITORIAL DIRECTOR
Ellie Atkinson

SENIOR EDITORS
Brett Hill, Grace Dahl

PRESS STAFF
Zoie Dinehart, Allison Lange, Sophie McPherson, Kylie Newton, Ava Willett

For Aaron

CONTENTS

III. The Stick Tries to Understand the Hands

IV. The Cup Tries to Understand the Hands

I.

The Stone Tries to Understand the Hands

I had not thought *shape* or
comfort or even *smooth*.
I had not noticed myself
as singular. But their caress said *you*
in a way that the ocean's
never did. They held me with
a different kind of hunger.
In that engulfing I felt somehow
more of myself, not less.
I understood how specific
the world could be.

Scavenger Hunt

I wanted to be that thorough,
so I collected the light in your face

as you held up each rock
you had found: this one

with the hole at the center,
this one with the surprising green.

I know that faces light up more
at some things than at others. Love is about

selection, which makes it unfair.
Add this to the collection: how beautiful

that disparity, how fervently we long
for that particular injustice.

I Didn't Know

I didn't know I loved my knees
until I curled up into the
strange loneliness of childhood
and found them there waiting for me.
I pressed them to my lips and said,
nice to meet you. They smelled like
their own wet-earth selves
and it was clear they had no interest
in impressing me. *We've been here
all along*, they said, and I sat
breathing in the discovery of their
artless, reliable company.

DMZ

At first they were not even letters but
sounds that made up a name: dee em zee,
a political cabaret, which is to say
a collection of responses
to the world at the time. I saw it on
posters and ticket stubs before I saw it
in the newspaper: *The DMZ*,
which meant to me and therefore fixed
in my mind the feeling of entering a space
and standing quiet and singular next to the
adults. The sense of an interior,
coming into a dark bar from the daylight,
the effort to make something out of the
detritus around you. I knew the response but not
the origin, didn't understand that war or
the others, the rivers and rice paddies
or the kitchens and bedrooms throughout
our own country. I still don't know what a DMZ is,
not really. I don't know how to create a zone
of neutrality, where people agree to
hold off or hold back. I don't know
how people fight or stop fighting.
What is the zone in anyone's house or country—
that word *demarcation*. How it gets done.
You walk down the block in any July
and the door to the synagogue is open
so the men's chanting spills all the way out.
Another sense of interior, the fervor and cadences
and some sense of the way their throats
are holding something that goes all the way back
to a time when survival was not guaranteed. As it never is.
I did learn something about responding
but that doesn't mean I know how to make
the necessary space now. There are so many letters I
hold in my mouth.

Watergate

This summer the family
stays inside. Hour after hour
the television glows with
betrayals and excuses
of guilty men. Clearly
the reign of easy faith
has ended. Staccato
as rain on the roof,
the bedroom voices
beat out their own drama
as tedious and terrifying
as the nation's. In the next room
the child at the window
breathes in the mesh of the screen
and through it the air of the
sodden, disbelieving world.

Portrait of the Artist as Some Kind of Scholar

Heat within heat, ovens
in the city in July

at an age when pizza itself was
an occasion of mathematical

joy. On the wall of photos
an actor my father knew

which taught me the habit
of glancing over to find that photo

each time we arrived. Like finding the place
on the map, the point of recognition.

Like the men two generations before
who went out summer evenings

to the corner where they knew they'd find
others from the same *old country*—

Houston and Essex, Essex and Delancey,
each intersection a graph of desire

because we are   maybe   what we long for
or what we recognize. Heat

within heat, desire within a body.
The flute player I saw each time I

walked in the park decades later,
stripped to his essential

body, practicing in the sun.
I'm talking about devotion.

What interests me is
how things get made.

What are you doing here

Once I walked into a prison
and then out again. Once my arms were bare
in a neighborhood where every other woman
was covered. Once I sat in a room with people who
had suffered in ways I had never.
Once I was the only one in the theatre
who didn't want to be on stage. There's no
getting around it, how audacious and specific
I have been.

The Apple Speaks

The truth is I wanted them
to choose me. Disobedience, yes,
but maybe something else—fealty
to the complication of their own
bodies, the problem
of curiosity: taste and see, taste and
find out. Before, I mattered only as much
as everything else. Now,
I mattered more. They made me
myself and they made me part of them,
and in this new disturbance
we were ripe and full of our
desire to know what came next.

The Other Apple Speaks

It just so happened that
I was the one who caught
his attention, falling
as I did and as we all
do—yes he too and everyone
like him—and surely he had
noticed it before,
how something compels
us toward each other,
and by *us* I mean any of us,
every object attracting every
other object with a force proportional
to the product of the two masses,
meaning that it matters who or what
is falling. But there will always be
that sweet inevitability, each to
the other, and inversely proportional
to the square of the distance between them,
meaning it matters where they start from
and the space they travel to come
together. But still
he must have known this before,
felt it in his gut or feet or heart, known
at least that he was subject to it,
known that *something* was happening
even before he began trying to understand
exactly what and why and how.

Gravity

I forgot I had a body
because the sky was so
full of its own blueness
and I thought maybe I could be
blue like that and

later there were more stars than
feelings so I thought maybe
I could be starry like that
and

          it's not true,
what I told you just now.
I didn't forget. I couldn't.
The longing itself was
the reminder—
belly, spine, lungs, heartbeat—
the weight of it so
actual and inevitable that I was
bound by law to remember.

What They Did

Taught me how to arrive every morning
not exactly ready for it but full
of whatever the feeling is when it seems
inevitable, like something that just happens and happens
until it seems like one more aspect of the spinning earth.
Dragged is what the time did and what they did to
my body against the carpet of our nursery school floor each
morning, maybe only because or maybe not even because
they wanted to but maybe simply because they could
fit their hands around my narrow wrists and pull
like the handle of a toy wagon or sled and I am not presuming
anything about their natures or futures because we were only
children but the thing is the teachers who taught me
that people can see but not know or know but not see in the given
instance and the other thing is that all this time later when
someone rubs their feet against a carpet in just that way
it makes me shiver and cringe and it makes me say *stop*.

What We Did

It wasn't a matter of *could*
(like you learn in psychology class
about how *any of us*
could do that).

                 It was a matter of *did*,
we did, *I* did. I did look
at the look on her face, the wanting
to get away, and knew that I
caused it, with my friend, in the woods,
because we brought the neighbor girl there
and teased and mocked her and yes I am aware
of how much worse it could have been,
how many worse things happen
in I don't know how many woods,
but this one was mine, this
ceremony among the trees
where I said *I do* like some
reluctant, inevitable bride
who says yes I will take this
possibility of cruelty and join with it
as my own
                so that later, much later,
when someone says I love you
they will have to be loving this too.

II.

The Glass Tries to Understand the Hands

At first I thought mostly about the job
I had to do: getting between them
and staying there. Let nothing pass
from one to the other—I with the certainty
of my literal body. It took me time
to understand how incarnate
imagination can be
and how necessity mothers
this kind of invention.
I was supposed to prevent it but
I know what I felt. At each goodbye
their heat bloomed through me
and it was not because I suddenly turned
porous or derelict—no, I promise
I did what I was made to do
and what was in my nature. But
if you ask what happened
in the makeshift gesture
my presence required, if I am
honest in my accounting I admit I
would have to call it touch.

Angels

The snow let us warm it
that day, which is to say
that it allowed our bodies
to influence it, which is sometimes
what bodies do. They change things

so that even afterward
there is (there remains)
that joyful, ruinous imprint.

Come with me into the great hall

where the dinosaurs still rise
toward the ceiling, filling the room
like declarative sentences,
just the fact of them astounding us.
Each rib embraces an empty space,
telling us nothing about
their lumbering bodies, or heat, or
beating hearts. This is what we will have to
invent, or at least reassemble. I used to
walk past them in the dark each morning
before anyone else arrived. I used to be young.
I used to marvel that it was a choice
and not a requirement
to clothe our skeletons with desire
and enter the world so fully. Or to stay there.
Yes, especially that. There is so much to see
in this great hall. I am asking you to come closer.

Theory of Mind

Because I had not been long
on this earth, I asked my father
why the sign said the name
of our street. I told him we already knew
what street it was.
He was gentle when he explained
that not all the other people knew
what we knew.
And so the world split into
many minds, splintering like glass
or like that original division of cells
that made life, so it was let's say a kind of
birthing—and yes, how startling that new
solitude
            but also how tantalizing, maybe,
to have this new prospect:
now it would no longer be obvious
but instead astonishing
when one of those other minds
managed—tendril-like, bridge-like,
vibrating with curiosity and faith—
to make it across the ordinary chasm
and say, *yes I know what you mean.*

Captcha

Yes, I can attest to being
human, which means
I can enter this site where
things happen,
            some things,
       the things we are still trying
to understand.
            I know the poet said
I learn by going where I have to go.
I must therefore have had to go
to this site of strange reckoning,
determined to be more than a tourist
when we try to discover how to own
our own hands, how to live
in the hardscrabble country of
can't take it back.
            I know I said
I would join you here, week after week
trying to map out the space between
then and now. We had a job to do
and we did it, more or less
willingly, going where we had to go.

            I know the playwright said
I am human and nothing human is
alien to me. I can attest to it
now, the heat in the
armpits, the naked confessions,
the years that it took. If I want
I can re-enter the site
where we tried to discover
how fire becomes glass,
how throat becomes say,
how reach becomes touch.

The Moon Considers the Prospect
of the First Lunar Mission in Fifty Years

They can come back
if they want to.

It's all right
with me.

I understand
the lure of it

(the way they are
always wanting

to know more)
and I too feel

the pull (how they try
to find themselves

in me) even if I seem
unchanged. I see how

they look at me
and I recognize

the way the longing
tugs at them (each time as if

the first time, the swell
and recede).

So they can come back
if they want to

but they should know
we are bound

regardless—
two bodies mesmerized

by the original astonishing
impact

from which we are both
still reeling.

At the Execution

Not the flower blooming outside
the prison walls. Not the stars
visible on the night they did it.
Not how blue the sky was
the morning after. Some other time,
maybe, a catalog of all that heedless,
persistent beauty, but not this poem,
not right now. Just the look on the faces
of the ones who tried to stop it
and how they allow themselves,
for a moment, to take each other's hands.

When the man across the park

broke off a branch of blossoms
and presented it to his daughter
as if it were his to give

my mother ran at him raging
this is not how it works.
These are here for all of us.

Maybe the man's daughter was thinking
how beautiful or *how loved I am*

(a child takes what is given
however it is given)

but my mother thought
stop, thief

and so I stood under
the bloom of her fury
and learned something about
protest and
restraint
(oh, to take those blossoms
as my own!)

which are maybe
in their own ways
also forms of love.

For the Record

I may have forgotten to tell you
about the letters I ate in
heaping spoonfuls
and how their noodle shapes
tumbled together on my tongue,
letting me know them for just that
while, so that I learned by
taste and feel, learned
by taste and feel how to read
what the world had to say

and I may have forgotten to tell you
how sweet and savory that process
was, how it gave me
what I needed, how no matter
whether I found it in sand or chalk,
finger tracings on window steam
or refrigerator magnets you could glide
like skaters, I would one day use
that rich, durable alphabet to
tell you about everything else.

The Experiment

We were painting the room and I
knocked over the can making the
paint spill onto the floor like sunrise
and so I said *all right* and
bent down to stick my hands into
that insolent dawn
so that I could be the paint as well as
myself and feel what it is like to be that
certain of my own blooming

I Could Say

I could say I love you the way the sky loves
the stars, because how would the sky recognize itself

without those fiery bodies that give it something
to contain? You could say the sky needs to keep

busy, holding all of that
aloft, and maybe just the holding is

enough; maybe it isn't necessary to know all of them
by name. It's hard, anyway, to think in numbers

big as that. We're always trying to say or show
how much. When I was littler than this

I crawled inside the cardboard box, empty after some home
delivery, and kept myself company by writing numbers

on its insides. I thought if I kept at it
I could break some record and count all the way

to the end, like a final destination
on a train ride, or a box you could crawl into

and say *at last*. Let's not live
there, but somewhere else where we have no idea

how many but we taste them as we go. Where I
write you on my insides. With indelible pen.

What You Did

Started with an onion. How
so many recipes begin, no matter
where you are in the world: first,
chop an onion. So you did that.
You took care of things
one meal at a time. By *things* I mean
me. You started with an onion
because of the way in chopping it
you have to hold your hands
just so. We didn't know
what would happen next. We said
a recipe for disaster, but how
did we mean the phrase? Maybe not only
that trouble is inevitable; maybe also
that there are things to do. Ask it
like this: what do you need now? And now?

III.

The Stick Tries to Understand the Hands

Is it violence or
curiosity, the way they tear

at my surfaces? How can this
prepare me for fire?

How strange, the
promise they make.

If I let them see
my greenest, wettest

self, is it really possible
that I will yield

something sweet?

In Person

Sitting in the same room after so long
      reminds us that bodies
can only be in one place at a time.

Over there in the corner
      imagination and poetry huddle together
and conspire to defy the laws

of singularity and loss,
      but life climbs in the open window,
makes itself comfortable and says

actually, only this. You can travel to the moon
      but you'll come back still holding
the knowledge that at any time

someone may break or leave or need to be
      buried in the earth. Keep sitting here
with that beating inside you. Life says

your fear doesn't trouble me.
      Fear is the way I know
you're paying attention.

This One Life

All summer I didn't go
because I didn't understand
how finite things are, how
there are chances and chances
and then no chances left.
I thought I had no place
at that bedside
or that I might fumble
whatever was handed to me

so instead I went into bed
and out again, I went into the city
for the sweet welcoming indifference
of its breakfasts and alleyways and
the lattice of streets that said
you decide, and met friends
to talk as though we could decide
about sadness: go deeper in or
farther away? We liked
just that degree of distance

between us: a table,
some cups, a pad of paper,
the stories the mothers said
not to write. We stepped in
and out of our lives as though
the point was the choice,
leaving the party to sit on the steps
in the sweet welcoming indifference
of the night air and returning
as if nothing had happened.
And then I came home to the news
that there was no more news to wait for

and I held the phone tight
in the only hands I had.

Sitting at this kind of bedside

you will eventually get restless, need
coffee, want to see something else.
If you step outside, the blossoms
will be both an affront and a blessing.
Life will keep insisting on itself
because that's what it does. You'll want
to stay there under the trees
and also go back inside
where the sadness is happening.
You'll feel this dilemma as long as
your own heart is beating.

The Anticipation

When it's time for loss,
it might not be
bearable. I dare you
to praise this. Yes,
this: the fist around your heart
saying how? How will you
survive it? An extravagance of
blossoms, olives, more salt
than we need—someday, afterward,
all these pleasures will
complicate grief. You can't count on
purity, but praise that too:
how messy things become.
By *things* I mean love. Go ahead
and say it. The tether, the binding
that makes loss so unthinkable. Praise
how we want to hoard
what we're given, wrap ourselves
around it and defy anyone to
tell us to let go. But we'll
have to. It's how it works.
You don't have to
praise that, but praise how
we protest. How we try
not to think about it.
How we sit at this table
sucking the meat from the bone,
knowing the thief will come.

Arrhythmia

is when the heart's impulses
become erratic, and this is not
a metaphor, this is just one of the things
that can happen to a body. If in that
syncopation I see a demonstration
of how much can go wrong, that's just
me wanting to make something of it.
When we talk about the heart we mean
all kinds of things. You meant to tell me
what it's like to feel such offbeat
fear and how you managed to set it right
with Bach, bananas, sunlight, and
some kind of submission to
the mystery of things. So if I see
in that list some kind of illustration
of how you and I have always tried
to assemble from the vast scatter of the world
a list of what can make a difference—
well, that's just me doing what I do.
Pointing things out. Because
even before we understood that hearts
could falter in this particular way,
we were already keeping track of ways
to remind them how to do what they know
how to do. So if we sometimes
need to make use of those
reminders now, that would not have to be
a metaphor, just a fact about the heart
and what it takes to keep it steady. Steady on.

Elegy for the Rough Draft

Praise the way it gave itself
up, first onto the dance floor,
ready and willing to be
anyone's fool. Praise how it forgot
an umbrella, grabbed clothes
that don't match, dumped
scraps onto the table,
let's see what we've got.
Yes, praise the self-
love that allowed for such
daring, but praise also the
hunger, the underbelly, the
soft and the raw.
Praise the rough draft
for saying not only
this is what I am but also
this is what I need.

Thrift (in Wartime)

All day you were careful.
You walked to the store,
ladled your share of milk
from the can, roasted
chickpeas and called it
coffee, didn't admit to
wanting more. Only with
the constellations did you
allow it: *how manifold*
are thy works, O Lord,
turning yourself to them
at the window each night,
your body a dipper of desire
for an unrationed sky.

Now I can say

I wanted it—
the horse small enough to appear
in my cupped hands

or later the boy, the publisher,
the winning ticket, the experience
of something happening, something

singular and distinguishing and above all
coveted. I can say now that I know how it feels
to sit in the corner of that dark bar of envy

and how the wishing leaves its own handprints
on your body. So many times I did not outrun
disappointment, but lay there sprawled on its

sodden ground, looking up at desire
the way a child on the floor at a family dinner
looks up at every unholy underside

of the furniture, the ceiling, the bodies all
around her, those unbeautiful facts of her life
that she could not learn any other way.

Letter

Dear wanting, I
understand a few things
now. In a way I have loved you
from the start

but I thought ours was
a private romance
like the way the child outside
in her own sleeping bag
falls in love with the stars
and keeps it to herself

(does not talk about
how the largeness fills her)

so I didn't realize we could be like
the pianist and the keys,
the acrobat and trapeze,
the tulip and the sun—
so unabashed in their coupling,
so public with their vows.

Dear wanting, I didn't realize
we could step out into the world
together, and dance.

Somebody did

remember to lock the door.
Somebody did think to look in the address book.
Somebody did make the calls.
Somebody did notice the dog needed to go out.
Somebody did cancel the appointment.
Somebody did throw out the sour milk
eventually. Somebody did say it was strange
to see the hair still in the brush and
the crumbs on the table. Somebody did keep
track of time. Somebody did put the dishes away.

IV.

The Cup Tries to Understand the Hands

After a while I began to
expect—no, if I'm honest I'll say
I began to long for that
claiming, the way they insisted
that it matters how you start things
and that taste is itself a kind of
praise of the actual world.
I longed for their faith and I
found it, because
they did come for me
again and again. Each day
they came reaching with their
yes this morning as well as
all the others, their *yes this again*
even though, even when—
their *I will choose*
how I am going to live.

The Uses of Doubt

You call for faith. I show you doubt, to prove that faith exists.

—Robert Browning

To provoke the world into showing you
in as many ways as you need:

the crocus opening itself to the bee,
the skydiver believing in the parachute,

and for that matter, anyone who
takes off their clothes in front of

anyone else, or schedules next year's
appointment, or steps onto a frozen lake.

By these arguments, faith is everywhere.
When I went to prison

to visit a man who'd been there
thirty years, he swore to me

he wouldn't die there.
I thought I would learn from him

how to want without
getting, or what a man could do

with only those walls. I figured
he needed to believe what

he needed to believe. But then he got out,
tumbling through that peculiar passage

with all of us waiting like stunned midwives,
and so I learned something different

about doubt, and belief. These days
what I try to do is offer myself

in my own display of ardent provocation
so that the world might show me. Show me again.

On the Carousel

When I bought my fourth ticket
      the man said, *you must really love*

horses. Horses? My throat was full
      of wonder. How did he not see

that without sweat or whinny or
      open field, this had to be

about something else. The music,
      sure, but even more than that the faces

of the parents each time as we came
      whirling back around, how they waited

and watched for us with the routine astonishment
      of earth encountering again the yes

of sunrise—this was what I loved enough
      to come back and back for. I wanted to deliver

that reassurance (or to receive it):
      here we are and are and are.

Young at Least for Now

In a languid hurry,
both smarter and dumber
than we will be again,
we walk 'til our feet blister
and sit 'til the coffee mugs
smudge with cinnamon and
lipstick and foam. Heraclitus
tells us we can't step into
the same river twice
and we don't. We are new again
with each thing we say and
each glance at the mirror.
But Heraclitus, what is the word
for the way we can't help wanting to
cup our hands in that river
and drink it, keep it, turn it into
something inside us that abides?

You Have to Make a Decision Sometimes

At the sushi bar
I said yes to
what was offered
because I wanted
the briefest occasion
of joy, but
again and again,
not just the one time,
and also of course
the skillful hands—

but really what I
wanted most was
to have to
trust someone
that much.

The Trade

You were there at the
edge of the world, about to
board the ship that would take you
away, and to. The local rabbi
gave you his blessing. *Why not?*
you might have thought. *Take
what help you can get.*
But when another passenger
offered to buy that blessing from you,
you took the coins from his hand.
There are so many ways to make
the crossing. Which man was more
cunning, or which the greater fool?
How could anyone know
what those coins would do?
You waited three weeks,
rocking with them
as they bore into your hand
like salt, like thirst. When you arrived
you must have seen
they had left an imprint there
like a map of your new faith.

One of the first things I noticed

was that I was now in love
with the wheelbarrow yes the
redness of it and the wheel
barrow of it like nothing else
in the world but also like
everything else I had ever
noticed and therefore said
look look at this

and truth be told
(which I am telling here)
I wanted now to put my hands
on that glaze of rain
water and count how many white
chickens and then go on to tell
the poet that I was in love
with him for giving me
this scene upon which
so much depends
and maybe even go on to
love myself for still being full
of so much loving.

Remember *Waiting?*

The sprawled languor of it,
so when that song came on the radio
it was as if your own fervor had
made it happen. All that lying on the bed
rehearsing what you would do if
the moment did come,
all that watching the actors in rehearsal
doing the scene again and again.
And then on opening night
there are no guarantees because
that's what it means to be *live*. No matter
the hours of practice; none of them has ever
been right here until now. Neither have you.
At the party afterward you watch them all
through song after song until
the leading man says
come and dance, kid. He offers
an option and you take it because
that's what it means to be *going*,
which is a synonym for having a heart that
beats out a tempo, or for
breathing, or for entering into
some kind of agreement with
the life that is all around you.

Because the world is sometimes unbearably large

we decided to become a sonnet or a birdcage
so we would have something to climb into.
We found a way to make things small enough
or at least contained enough
to understand. This was something to do
with our bodies, and a good thing, a useful thing.
Like making a cup with your hands
to bring just that much rushing water
to your mouth. We decided to form ourselves
around the empty space the way the clay does
when it chooses *bowl* or *vase*. This was something
to do with our longing, and a good thing,
a useful thing. Like making a decision.
Like making some kind of home.

Again

It was amazing and amazing and again amazing
that it was morning again, the lovers turning over
in their beds and finding each other
again here again you again still good
morning and even when they let themselves slip
into the ordinary shaking the
coffee grounds into the compost packing
the lunch finding the right shoes heading out
into the outside day—
                    even then the slipping was itself
amazing, because it meant that it was possible
to rest themselves in the daily *yes*, the taking it
for granted, this morning as all the others,
like the skater who trusts the lake to
hold again this time.

Why I Stay

Because we are delicious together.
Because we know how to turn taste
into meaning. Because we don't mind
that each breakfast starts it all over again,
the need to decide what to do about
hunger. Because it's hard to cook an egg
just right and doesn't really get
any easier with time, but somehow
you learn to live with that situation.
Because even if you say *pungent* or
bitter or *buttery* or *smooth*
there is no useful word for taste.
Only taste really understands taste
and can talk about it. You know
how it is—no one else
truly knows what goes on
inside a relationship. Add some
having to the wanting. Stir.

I survived by

punctuating the
sentences in front of me
because the commas told me
when to breathe and the periods
taught how to take one thing
at a time and the semicolons
said we can be separate but also
joined and the parentheses
were a comfort of enclosure

and together all of them said
give it over, the sometimes too much
of your life, the this this and that,
the that that that that—

give it so it can be
given back to you
sturdy enough and
maybe even clear.

What to Say

Sometimes there is nowhere to go
but the shelter of our own need

to believe in a way to care for each
other, remembering how we do that

when we need to. That's what I said
when I had to say something

about how to tell a child that people do
terrible things to other people sometimes.

I said tell her we do know   we do still know
how to care for each other afterward.

Is the sky an example? No, but looking at it is.
I mean one person pointing out the specific beauty

to another, that could be an example, yes. But not
the birch tree or the wren or the mountain range,

not all by themselves. We are talking here about
human hands and what they can do.

Someone will find the right vase for the flowers.
Someone will have started those flowers from seed.

How Are You Now?

When I said I am more loved
than I even knew
I meant I am dappled—
not exactly in the manner of
the horse flank or forest floor
but still like the light saying
look what shines through.
Look what canopy this kind of joy
can make out of the spaces between.

Sometimes too I am the egg
broken open, the road in mud season. I am
face up and allowing. I am soaking everything in.

What I Did

I stepped outside to see what
the sky was up to. I cracked an egg
into a bowl. I looked again
at my lover's face. It was time
for breakfast. I had a brief affair
with the coffee until I remembered
it was actually my lover who gave it to me
so there was nothing furtive
about the pleasure. We talked
about who would cook dinner.
I glanced out the window
and caught the fleet of cyclists
streaming round the corner.
I appreciated the birds without knowing much
about birds. I finished the coffee.
I thought, if I am lucky
I will do this again tomorrow. In other words
I found a way to stay there, right in the center of
my life. Tell me if you have any better ideas.

ACKNOWLEDGMENTS

I am grateful to the following journals in which several of the poems in this book first appeared (sometimes in earlier versions). I am also grateful to those who responded to the work in progress: Rosebud Ben-Oni for her wise suggestions about the shape of the manuscript; Eric McHenry for his 2019 workshop at the Bear River Writers' Conference, in which I developed this book's title poem and the whole idea of poems written in the voice of objects encountering human hands; the wonderful friends and faculty who have helped make Bear River my poetry home over these many years; Joy Gaines-Friedler and Elizabeth Solsburg, draft readers extraordinaire, who keep Bear River going for me all year round.

Beloit Poetry Journal: "This One Life"

Briar Cliff Review: "I Didn't Know"

Connecticut River Review: "DMZ"

Diode: "Elegy for the Rough Draft," "For the Record"

Dunes Review: "Come with me into the great hall," "How Are You Now?"

Ginosko Literary Journal: "Thrift (in Wartime)," "At the Execution"

Grist: A Journal of the Literary Arts: "Angels," "What I Did"

Inscape: "Arrhythmia"

Mud Season Review: "Again"

One Art Poetry Journal: "What to Say"

Panoplyzine: "The Anticipation "

Poet Lore: "The Stone Tries to Understand the Hands," "The Glass Tries to Understand the Hands"

Sixth Finch: "Scavenger Hunt," "In Person"

Tar River Poetry: "Letter" (first published as "Dear Wanting"), "The Uses of Doubt"

Thimble Literary Magazine: "The Moon Considers the Prospect of the First Lunar Mission in Fifty Years"

Typehouse: "The Apple Speaks"

In the process of turning the manuscript into a book, I am grateful to Cornerstone Press's dedicated team: publisher Dr. Ross Tangedal, editors Grace Dahl and Kylie Newton, proofreaders Ellie Atkinson and Brett Hill, and production director Allison Lange. I appreciate Cornerstone's commitment to writers, and to the students who, through their work at the press, join the community of those who love and care about book publishing.

SUSANNAH SHEFFER is the author of *Break and Enter* (2021) and *This Kind of Knowing* (2013), and her poems have appeared in a wide variety of print and online journals. For many years she taught writing workshops for teenagers and now works as a clinical mental health counselor and a writer and researcher focusing on people affected by the death penalty. She lives with her husband in Western Massachusetts.